REAL-LIFE
SCIENTIFIC
ADVENTURES

APOLLO 11 AND THE FIRST MEN ON THE MOON

ERIC KEPPELER

PowerKiDS
press™

New York

Published in 2019 by The Rosen Publishing Group, Inc.
29 East 21st Street, New York, NY 10010

First Edition

Editor: Theresa Morlock
Book Design: Reann Nye

Photo Credits: Cover, p. 1 NASA/Science Source/Getty Images; p. 4 Mark Sutton/EyeEm/Getty Images; p. 5 Steve Bronstein/Stone/Getty Images; p. 6 National Archives/Hulton Archive/Getty Images; p. 7 (left) Harold M. Lambert/Archive Photos/Getty Images; pp. 7 (right), 8, 9, 11, 14, 15 (both), 17, 23 (bottom), 27 (top), 28, 29 Courtesy of NASA; p. 10 https://commons.wikimedia.org/wiki/File:Aldrin.jpg; p. 12 https://commons.wikimedia.org/wiki/File:Michael_collins.jpg; pp. 13, 27 (bottom) Bettmann/Getty Images; p. 18 Space Frontiers/Archive Photos/Getty Images; pp. 19, 20, 21, 22, 24 NASA/Hulton Archive/Getty Images; p. 23 (top), 25 NASA/Science Source/Getty Images; p. 26 https://en.wikipedia.org/wiki/File:Apollo_11.jpg.

Library of Congress Cataloging-in-Publication Data

Names: Keppeler, Eric, author.
Title: Apollo 11 and the first men on the moon / Eric Keppeler.
Description: New York : PowerKids Press, [2019] | Series: Real-life scientific adventures | Includes bibliographical references and index.
Identifiers: LCCN 2017050392| ISBN 9781508168423 (library bound) | ISBN 9781508168447 (pbk.) | ISBN 9781508168454 (6 pack)
Subjects: LCSH: Project Apollo (U.S.)–Juvenile literature. | Apollo 11 (Spacecraft)–Juvenile literature. | Space flight to the moon–Juvenile literature.
Classification: LCC TL789.8.U6 A5429 2019 | DDC 629.45/4–dc23
LC record available at https://lccn.loc.gov/2017050392

Manufactured in the United States of America

CPSIA Compliance Information: Batch #CS18PK: For Further Information contact Rosen Publishing, New York, New York at 1-800-237-9932

CONTENTS

EARTH'S NEAREST NEIGHBOR

Have you ever looked up at the moon and wondered what it would be like to be there? It's very different from Earth, and it's very far away.

Scientists think Earth's moon was formed about 4.5 billion years ago. It's an average of about 238,000 miles (383,023 km) away from Earth, and it's only about a quarter as large as our planet. Because it's so much smaller, the gravity is much less than on Earth, so everything weighs less than it does here.

EXPEDITION REPORT

Days on the moon are very long—about 708 hours. That means it gets very hot during the day—as hot as 273°Fahrenheit (134°Celsius). It can be as cold as -243°Fahrenheit (-153°Celsius) at night.

Anyone can look at the moon, but only 12 men can say they've actually been there.

Only 12 people, all Americans, have ever set foot on the moon. The first **mission** to reach the moon left Earth on July 16, 1969, with three men on board. This was the Apollo 11 mission.

RACE TO THE MOON

People have been interested in the moon for thousands of years, but the real space race began in the 1950s when two rival nations—the United States and the Soviet Union—tried to see who could get there first.

The Soviets put the first **satellite**, called *Sputnik 1*, into Earth orbit in 1957. They made the first craft (*Luna 2*) to reach the moon two years later. In 1961, Yuri Gagarin became the first man in space. A month later, Alan Shepard became the first American in space, and John Glenn

EXPEDITION REPORT

In a famous speech on September 12, 1962, U.S. President John F. Kennedy challenged the American space agency NASA to put a man on the moon and return him safely home before the end of the decade.

became the first American to orbit Earth in 1962.

The early U.S. space program had three stages.
The Mercury rockets carried astronauts into space, and
the Gemini rockets helped them learn to **maneuver**. The
Apollo rockets went to the moon.

7

NEIL ARMSTRONG

All the astronauts wanted to be included on the first mission to land on the moon. NASA had a tough choice but finally picked Neil Armstrong, Edwin "Buzz" Aldrin, and Michael Collins on January 6, 1969. All three were experienced astronauts.

Armstrong, the mission commander, was born August 5, 1930, in Ohio. He was a Navy flier, a test pilot, and an engineer. Armstrong was a very talented pilot. He flew more than 200 different types of aircraft, including jets, rockets, and helicopters.

Armstrong and fellow astronaut Dave Scott flew the Gemini 8 mission in 1966. Armstrong performed the first successful docking, or connecting, of two **vehicles** in space, which would be an important step for the Apollo rockets.

8

This photo was taken by Neil Armstrong. You can see his shadow in the bottom left corner of the picture.

BUZZ ALDRIN

Aldrin, the **lunar module** pilot, was born January 20, 1930, in New Jersey. He was a fighter pilot in the Air Force and flew 66 combat, or battle, missions during the Korean War. He also had an engineering **degree**.

Aldrin and fellow astronaut Jim Lovell flew the Gemini 12 mission—the last flight in the Gemini program—on a four-day trip in November 1966. During that mission, Aldrin set a new record for spending time outside a ship in just a spacesuit. He took part in a five-and-a-half-hour spacewalk.

By the time he left NASA in 1971, Aldrin had spent 289 hours and 53 minutes in space—including 7 hours and 52 minutes of spacewalk time. That's more than an entire day at school spent on a spacewalk!

Buzz Aldrin was the lunar module pilot for Apollo 11 and the second man to set foot on the moon.

MICHAEL COLLINS

Collins was born October 31, 1930, in Italy while his father was stationed there. Collins was an Air Force flier and a test pilot with about 5,000 hours of flying time. He tried to become an astronaut in 1962, but he wasn't chosen. He didn't give up, and NASA picked him to be an astronaut the next year.

Collins and astronaut John Young flew the Gemini 10 mission on a three-day trip in July 1966. He performed a successful docking with another vehicle, and he also went for a spacewalk, moving outside his ship for more than an hour.

By the time Collins left NASA in 1970, he had spent 266 hours in space. This includes the time he spent with the Gemini 10 and Apollo 11 missions.

Michael Collins remained on *Columbia* to make sure the Apollo 11 crew could get safely back to Earth after the others landed on the moon.

TRAINING

Being an astronaut is hard work, and you have to be in great shape. Early astronauts needed to be younger than 40 years old and shorter than 5-foot-11 (1.8 m) so they could fit comfortably into the tiny **space capsule**. They needed a degree in engineering and had to be good pilots with at least 1,500 hours of flying time.

But training for the mission to the moon was even more challenging. Besides learning all the rocket controls, the astronauts had to learn how to survive in very hot and

EXPEDITION REPORT

Being an astronaut can be very dangerous. On January 27, 1967, during a **routine** practice, a capsule caught fire and killed Apollo 1 astronauts Gus Grissom, Roger Chaffee, and Ed White. Scientists learned from the accident to make new rockets safer.

Astronauts trained underwater so they could get used to moving more easily in their bulky spacesuits. It also helped them get used to the lower gravity on the moon and zero gravity in space.

cold places—just in case they landed in a place like that by accident.

They also had to practice flying the lunar module, which had been built to land on the moon. It wasn't like anything they'd flown before.

ROCKET LAUNCH

After years of training and practice, Armstrong, Aldrin, and Collins finally got their chance to go to the moon. Apollo 11 was **launched** at 9:32 a.m. July 16, 1969, at the Kennedy Space Center in Florida. More than 250,000 people watched the launch from the beaches and areas near the launchpad.

The giant engines on the first two stages of the rocket burned out and fell back to Earth after pushing the crew out into space. The third stage powered the astronauts to the moon.

It took 75 hours and 56 minutes for the rocket to reach orbit around the moon. Collins stayed in the command module, called *Columbia*, while Armstrong and Aldrin got into the lunar module, called *Eagle*, and flew it to the surface of the moon.

EXPEDITION REPORT

One of the most powerful machines ever built, the Saturn V rocket was 363 feet (110.6 m) tall—about the same height as a 36-story building and 60 feet (18.3 m) taller than the Statue of Liberty. It weighed 6.2 million pounds (2.8 million kg) when fully loaded.

16

The powerful **Saturn V** rocket, shown here, carried the astronauts to the moon.

TOUCH AND GO

As the astronauts flew closer to the surface of the moon, alarms started going off on *Eagle*. The people helping to guide the rocket from mission control in Houston, Texas, had to learn quickly if it was a problem that would make them stop the landing. They found a problem with

Eagle's computer, but it wouldn't keep them from landing.

But soon, Armstrong and Aldrin saw that *Eagle* wasn't where it was supposed to be. They were lost! Armstrong had to find a new place to land that wasn't rocky. With Aldrin counting down how much fuel they had left, Armstrong found a nice soft spot to set down just as *Eagle* was about to run out of fuel.

The lunar module, *Eagle*, could not land on a rocky field or near a big hole in the ground. It needed a flat area.

ONE SMALL STEP

At 4:18 p.m. July 20, the astronauts landed in an area on the moon called the Sea of **Tranquility**. "The *Eagle* has landed," Armstrong told everyone at mission control in Houston, and people all around the world began to celebrate the successful landing.

It took Armstrong and Aldrin several hours to get into their bulky spacesuits, and it was more than six hours before they finally opened the hatch and Armstrong started down the ladder.

He first set foot on the moon at 10:56 p.m., saying one of the most famous lines in human history: "That's one small step for a man, one giant leap for mankind." Aldrin followed him out about 20 minutes later to become the second man on the moon.

20

Millions of people around the world watched the live black-and-white images on their television sets as Armstrong became the first man to set foot on the moon.

FIRST LOOK

Since the gravity on the moon is so much less than on Earth, it was easier for the astronauts to move around. In their spacesuits, they weighed 360 pounds (163.3 kg) on Earth, but on

A view of Earth from the moon.

the moon they weighed just 60 pounds (27.2 kg)! "We're like two bug-eyed boys in a candy store," Armstrong said.

Aldrin agreed. He looked at the surface and said it was beautiful. The astronauts told the scientists back on Earth that the surface was powdery and that they could see their own footprints. They also set up a TV camera so that people back on Earth could see what it was like on the moon.

"It's like much of the high desert areas of the United States," Armstrong said. "It's different, but it's pretty out here."

The astronauts left footprints on the moon. The prints may still be there, since there is no wind on the moon.

EXPLORING

Armstrong and Aldrin spent two hours and 31 minutes exploring the surface of the moon, covering an area of about 2,691 square feet (250 sq m). They collected about 47.8 pounds (21.7 kg) of moon rocks to bring back to Earth for study.

The astronauts planted an American flag and left behind a mission patch from Apollo 1 in memory of their fallen comrades. They also left a plaque that read: "Here men from the planet Earth first set foot upon the moon. July 1969 A.D. We came in peace for all mankind."

After spending more than 21.5 hours on the moon, Armstrong and Aldrin lifted off at 1:54 p.m. July 21 to meet Collins. They then began the three-day journey back home to Earth.

Armstrong and Aldrin spent more than two hours walking on the moon. They quickly learned that bunny hops were the easiest way to travel in the light gravity.

COMING HOME AS HEROES

The astronauts of Apollo 11 made it back home in about three days, with the mission lasting a little more than 195 hours. Parachutes gently dropped the capsule into the Pacific Ocean at 12:50 p.m. July 24, and it was then recovered by the aircraft carrier USS *Hornet*.

The three astronauts were kept **isolated** for three weeks, in case they had picked up any unknown diseases during their trip. After they were released, they were honored in parades in many cities, including New York, Chicago, and Los Angeles. They were also awarded the Presidential Medal of Freedom by U.S. President Richard Nixon.

Aldrin, Armstrong, and Collins then went on a world tour and visited 25 other countries, meeting with leaders and being honored for what they had done.

The *Apollo 11* capsule splashed down into the Pacific Ocean southwest of Hawaii.

The *Apollo 11* astronauts were honored in parades around the world. Here, they wave to crowds in New York City.

MORE TRIPS TO THE MOON

Now that they knew how to do it, NASA sent more Apollo missions to the moon to try to learn as much as they could about Earth's nearest neighbor.

They also had a little fun. Apollo 14 astronaut Alan Shepard played golf on the moon, while Apollo 16 astronauts John Young and Charlie Duke drove a **lunar rover** on its surface.

Apollo 17 in 1972 was the last mission to the moon before the program ran out of money to build rockets.

EXPEDITION REPORT

Apollo 13 was launched April 11, 1970, carrying Jim Lovell, Fred Haise, and Jack Swigert. An explosion damaged their ship and kept them from landing on the moon, but the astronauts were able to return home safely.

Astronaut Gene A. Cernan (Apollo 17 commander) used the lunar rover to explore much more of the moon's surface.

No one has been there since. But now scientists have started thinking about the moon again. They may be able to start sending astronauts there again in the future. Would you like to be an astronaut and go to the moon?

MEN ON THE MOON

September 12, 1962

U.S. President John F. Kennedy challenges NASA to put a man on the moon and return him safely home before the end of the decade.

January 27, 1967

An Apollo 1 capsule is destroyed by a fire during a test on the launch pad, killing astronauts Gus Grissom, Ed White, and Roger Chaffee.

October 11, 1968

Apollo 7 is launched as a test flight in Earth orbit, carrying Wally Schirra, Donn Eisele, and Walter Cunningham.

December 21, 1968

Apollo 8 is launched and circles the moon, allowing Frank Borman, Jim Lovell, and Bill Anders to become the first to see the far side of the moon.

January 6, 1969

Neil Armstrong, Buzz Aldrin, and Michael Collins are told they will be the crew for Apollo 11.

March 3, 1969

Apollo 9 is launched, and Jim McDivitt, Dave Scott, and Russell Schweickart spend 10 days in Earth orbit conducting tests.

May 18, 1969

Apollo 10 is launched, carrying Tom Stafford, John Young, and Gene Cernan around the moon in a practice run for landing on the moon.

July 16, 1969

Apollo 11 is launched, carrying Neil Armstrong, Buzz Aldrin, and Michael Collins.

July 20, 1969

Neil Armstrong and Buzz Aldrin become the first two men to set foot on the moon.

July 21, 1969

Neil Armstrong and Buzz Aldrin take off from the moon.

July 24, 1969

The Apollo 11 crew returns to Earth.

April 11, 1970

Apollo 13 is launched carrying Jim Lovell, Fred Haise, and Jack Swigert. An accident keeps them from landing on the moon, but the astronauts returned home safely.

December 7, 1972

The last Apollo flight, 17, is launched, carrying Gene Cernan, Ron Evans, and Harrison Schmitt. Cernan and Schmitt landed on the moon.

degree: A title given to students when they complete a course of study at a college, university, or other school.

isolate: To put or keep something in a place that is separate from others.

launch: To officially start something. Also, to send a rocket or spacecraft into the sky.

lunar module: A small craft that carries astronauts from a rocket to the moon.

lunar rover: A vehicle that astronauts can drive on the moon.

maneuver: To make a series of changes in position and direction for a purpose.

mission: A specific task with which a group is charged.

routine: Commonplace; something done regularly.

satellite: A spacecraft placed in orbit around Earth, a moon, or a planet to collect information.

space capsule: A small spacecraft that is part of a larger spacecraft that holds instruments or crew.

tranquility: The state of being calm.

vehicle: A machine used to carry goods or people from one place to another.

INDEX

WEBSITES

Due to the changing nature of Internet links, PowerKids Press has developed an online list of websites related to the subject of this book. This site is updated regularly. Please use this link to access the list: www.powerkidslinks.com/rlsa/apollo